MW01615546

WOULD YOU RATHER?

CHRISTMAS EDITION

This book belongs to:

_____

Welcome! We hope you and your imagination are ready. As we go through this book together, we will be looking at many hilarious, thought-provoking, and conversation-starting Christmas-themed scenarios!

Playtime can now be fun and educational! Plus, you can take this game wherever you go: road trips, sleepovers, parties, and more!
Find out who has the better ideas and gives the best answers!

It is the perfect opportunity to develop critical thinking skills while having fun!

INSTRUCTIONS

1 The questions or "scenarios", in this game are divided in 2 sections, Christmas Eve and Christmas Day. That way, you can space out the game and have fun as a family all holiday!

2 two or more players are needed, along with a pencil to keep track of the winner of each round.

3 All the pages will have "Would You Rather" questions with two possible answers.

4 The youngest person will read the first question to start, but everyone can participate in taking turns reading later questions.

5 After the question is read aloud, the answering players answer as quickly as possible and give the reason for their decision.

INSTRUCTIONS

6
If someone doesn't answer fast enough, or picks both or no options, they don't get any points.

7
The player reading the question assigns 1 point to the best answer. Whoever gave the best answer wins for that question and the winner's name will be written in the box below the question.

8
Players will take turns reading the questions on the different pages, in order from youngest to oldest.

9
At the end, the Players tally up their own answers to figure out how many points they earned. Whoever gets the most points is the winner!

The most important rule is to be silly, creative, and have fun!

INDEX

CHRISTMAS EVE

Participants:

WOULD YOU RATHER

Have a carrot nose like Frosty the Snowman?

Have a red nose that glows like Rudolph the Reindeer?

Winner: | Points:

Q/1

WOULD YOU RATHER

Get to take a ride on Santa's sleigh?

Get to visit Santa's toy factory?

Winner: | Points:

Q/2

8

Participants:

WOULD YOU RATHER

Receive the perfect present from someone you love?

Give the perfect present to someone you love?

Winner: | Points:

Q 3

WOULD YOU RATHER

Have gumdrop buttons like the Gingerbread Man?

Have coal buttons like Frosty the Snowman?

Winner: | Points:

Q 4

Participants:

WOULD YOU RATHER

Learn how Santa can fit inside every chimney?

Learn how Santa can visit every home in the world in one night?

Winner:

Points:

Q/5

WOULD YOU RATHER

Open one huge present on Christmas Eve?

Open a bunch of little presents on Christmas Day?

Winner:

Points:

Q/6

Participants:

Q 7

WOULD YOU RATHER

Work with an elf who makes toys?

Work with an elf who makes shoes?

Winner: Points:

WOULD YOU RATHER

Be able to fly like one of Santa's reindeer?

Be able to live for hundreds of years like one of Santa's elves?

Winner: Points:

Q 8

Participants:

Q/9

WOULD YOU RATHER

Wear matching Christmas pajamas with your family?

Wear matching Santa hats and beards with your family?

Winner:

Points:

WOULD YOU RATHER

Open one really big present on Christmas?

Open five really small presents on Christmas?

Q/10

Winner:

Points:

Participants:

WOULD YOU RATHER

Spend Christmas Eve decorating
Christmas cookies?

Spend Christmas Eve watching a
Christmas movie?

Winner: Points:

Q 11

WOULD YOU RATHER

Spend a day with
the Grinch?

Spend a day with the
Abominable Snowman?

Winner: Points:

Q 12

13

Participants:

Q 13

WOULD YOU RATHER

Have three random days of school cancelled because of snow?

Have three nights of Christmas dinners?

Winner: Points:

WOULD YOU RATHER

Spend Christmas in the mountains covered in snow?

Spend Christmas out on the sand on a warm beach?

Q 14

Winner: Points:

Participants:

Q 15

WOULD YOU RATHER

Receive $30 as a
Christmas present?

Receive a random gift that
you didn't ask for?

Winner: Points:

WOULD YOU RATHER

Get to travel with Santa on his
sleigh, but never get any presents?

Get presents, but not get to meet
Santa and travel with him?

Q 16

Winner: Points:

Participants:

Q 17

WOULD YOU RATHER

Have a magic carrot nose that can bring a snowman to life?

Have a magic wand that can bring a toy to life?

Winner: | Points:

WOULD YOU RATHER

Have to eat 100 Christmas cookies?

Have to drink 10 glasses of eggnog?

Q 18

Winner: | Points:

16

Participants:

Q 19

WOULD YOU RATHER

Get a stocking
full of coal?

Get a stocking full
of dirty socks?

Winner: Points:

WOULD YOU RATHER

Sled down the biggest
hill in the world?

Have the biggest snowball
fight in the world?

Q 20

Winner: Points:

17

Participants:

Q 21

WOULD YOU RATHER

Build a small snow fort that lasted all winter?

Build a mansion-sized snow fort that lasts for one night?

Winner: | Points:

WOULD YOU RATHER

Get lost inside Santa's magic toy bag?

Get trapped inside a Christmas snow globe?

Winner: | Points:

Q 22

18

Participants:

WOULD YOU RATHER

Warm up with a cup of hot chocolate by the fire?

Warm up with roasted chestnuts by the fire?

Winner: | Points:

Q 23

WOULD YOU RATHER

Put marshmallows in your hot chocolate?

Put caramel syrup on your hot chocolate?

Winner: | Points:

Q 24

Participants:

WOULD YOU RATHER

Fight off a snow monster with a candy cane sword?

Fight off a dragon with a snowball canon?

Winner: Points:

Q 25

WOULD YOU RATHER

Live inside a giant snow globe?

Live inside a giant snow fort?

Winner: Points:

Q 26

Participants:

WOULD YOU RATHER

Share a room with an elf
who snores really loud?

Share a room with a reindeer
who is really smelly?

Winner: Points:

Q
27

WOULD YOU RATHER

Be able to know all the presents you
are going to get on Christmas?

Leave it all as
a surprise?

Winner: Points:

Q
28

Participants:

WOULD YOU RATHER

Grow a big white Santa beard
that you can't shave?

 or

Grow pointy elf ears?

Winner: Points:

Q 29

WOULD YOU RATHER

Buy a big
Christmas tree?

 or

Go into the forest and cut down
your own Christmas tree?

Winner: Points:

Q 30

Participants:

Q 31

WOULD YOU RATHER

Get to go trick-or-treating
on Christmas?

Get to open presents
on Halloween?

Winner: Points:

WOULD YOU RATHER

Not get any presents
on Christmas?

Have to eat the whole Christmas
meal by yourself?

Winner: Points:

Q 32

23

Participants:

Q 33

WOULD YOU RATHER

Be able to move one person you know to the Naughty List?

 or

Be able to move one person you know to the Nice List?

Winner: | Points:

WOULD YOU RATHER

Decorate 100 Christmas cookies?

 or

Wrap 100 Christmas presents?

Q 34

Winner: | Points:

Participants:

WOULD YOU RATHER

Celebrate Christmas many times a year?

Have every other holiday, but never have Christmas again?

Winner: Points:

Q / 35

WOULD YOU RATHER

Lose the ability to speak during Christmas?

Only be able to speak by singing Christmas songs?

Winner: Points:

Q / 36

Participants:

WOULD YOU RATHER

Have to wear Santa's red suit in the middle of summer?

Wear a bathing suit in the middle of a snowy winter?

Winner: Points:

Q 37

WOULD YOU RATHER

Live at the North Pole?

Live at the South Pole?

Winner: Points:

Q 38

Participants:

WOULD YOU RATHER

Be on the Naughty List for something that wasn't your fault?

Take someone else's spot on the Nice List?

Winner: | Points:

Q / 39

WOULD YOU RATHER

A sugar plum fairy fly out of your mouth every time you burp?

Tinsel come out of your nose every time you sneeze?

Winner: | Points:

Q / 40

Participants:

WOULD YOU RATHER

Have Gingerbread people the size of normal people live in your home?

 or

Be the size of a gingerbread person and live in a gingerbread house?

Winner: Points:

Q 41

WOULD YOU RATHER

Smell like a
reindeer?

 or

Look like
an elf?

Winner: Points:

Q 42

Participants:

Q 43

WOULD YOU RATHER

Have reindeer feet
like Rudolph?

Your nose glow like
Rudolph's nose?

Winner: Points:

WOULD YOU RATHER

Dress like Santa
every single day?

Dress like an elf
every single day?

Q 44

Winner: Points:

Participants:

WOULD YOU RATHER

Everything you eat
taste like candy canes?

Everything you drink taste
like hot chocolate (even water)?

Winner: | Points:

Q 45

WOULD YOU RATHER

Only be able to listen
to Christmas music?

Never listen to any
music ever again?

Winner: | Points:

Q 46

Participants:

WOULD YOU RATHER

Snow always be the
color yellow?

Snow always be
the color brown?

Winner: Points:

Q 47

WOULD YOU RATHER

Relive Christmas Day
every day?

Live every day as normal, but
Christmas Day gets skipped?

Winner: Points:

Q 48

Participants:

WOULD YOU RATHER

Have no Christmas decorations in your house?

Have no Christmas lights on your tree?

Winner:

Points:

Q 49

WOULD YOU RATHER

Bathe in Christmas jelly?

Bathe in eggnog?

Winner:

Points:

Q 50

CHRISTMAS DAY

Participants:

WOULD YOU RATHER

Get rid of a family Christmas tradition you don't like?

Get to choose a new family Christmas tradition?

Winner: | Points:

Q 51

WOULD YOU RATHER

The Easter Bunny be in charge of your presents?

The Tooth Fairy be in charge of your presents?

Winner: | Points:

Q 52

Participants:

WOULD YOU RATHER

Have to eat the entire Christmas ham all at once?

Never eat ham ever again?

Winner:

Points:

Q 53

WOULD YOU RATHER

Have fingers made out of candy canes?

Have teeth made out of marshmallows?

Winner:

Points:

Q 54

Participants:

WOULD YOU RATHER

Santa replace his reindeer
with flying cows?

Santa replace his reindeer
with flying snakes?

Winner: Points:

WOULD YOU RATHER

Be able to talk
to reindeer?

Be able to talk to
Christmas trees?

Winner: Points:

Participants:

WOULD YOU RATHER

Always smell like
a reindeer?

Be as hairy as the
abominable snow man?

Winner: Points:

Q 57

WOULD YOU RATHER

People think you are a Christmas
tree and try to decorate you?

People think you are a cookie
and try to munch you?

Winner: Points:

Q 58

Participants:

Q 59

WOULD YOU RATHER

Get a boring toy
for Christmas?

Get a toy that is alive, but it will only
talk to you about stocks and golf?

Winner:

Points:

WOULD YOU RATHER

Go mountain climbing with
Santa Claus?

Go surfing with
Mrs. Claus?

Q 60

Winner:

Points:

Participants:

WOULD YOU RATHER

Receive a present from
a dragon?

Receive a present
from a mermaid?

Q
61

Winner: Points:

WOULD YOU RATHER

Wear an ugly Christmas
sweater every day?

Q
62

All your regular clothes
be itchy?

Winner: Points:

Participants:

Q 63

WOULD YOU RATHER

Look for lost treasure with the Little Drummer Boy?

Go on vacation with Frosty the Snowman?

Winner: Points:

WOULD YOU RATHER

Stay home alone on Christmas when your family goes on vacation?

Your family invite everyone in the world to your house on Christmas?

Winner: Points:

Q 64

Participants:

WOULD YOU RATHER

Lose all of
your hair?

Have all your hair be made out of
Christmas tinsel?

Winner: Points:

Q 65

WOULD YOU RATHER

Receive a present
from a spider?

Receive a present from
a stinkbug?

Winner: Points:

Q 66

Participants:

WOULD YOU RATHER

Always get a papercut when you are wrapping presents?

Always burn your mouth when you are drinking hot chocolate?

Winner: Points:

Q 67

WOULD YOU RATHER

Accidentally melt Frosty the Snowman?

Accidentally burn down Santa's toy shop?

Winner: Points:

Q 68

Participants:

Q 69

WOULD YOU RATHER

Deck the halls with boughs of holly?

Rock around the Christmas tree?

Winner:

Points:

WOULD YOU RATHER

Have the same Christmas song stuck in your head forever?

Randomly start singing a Christmas song at least once a week?

Winner:

Points:

Q 70

Participants:

WOULD YOU RATHER

Have to buy a present
for a grouchy goblin?

Have to buy a present for
George Washington?

Winner: | Points:

Q 71

WOULD YOU RATHER

All of your clothes melt like snow
if it gets too hot?

All of your clothes be
permanently frozen?

Winner: | Points:

Q 72

Participants:

Q 73

WOULD YOU RATHER

Be trapped at an airport
on Christmas day?

Be stuck on a boat out
at sea on Christmas day?

Winner: Points:

WOULD YOU RATHER

Be a cat that gets a giant ball of
yarn for Christmas?

Be a bird that gets a giant
nest for Christmas?

Winner: Points:

Q 74

Participants:

Q 75

WOULD YOU RATHER

Only be able to see the Christmas colors (red and green)?

Be able to see every color except red and green?

Winner: Points:

WOULD YOU RATHER

Experience Christmas as a baby?

Experience Christmas as an elderly person?

Q 76

Winner: Points:

Participants:

Q 77

WOULD YOU RATHER

Design a brand-new toy with the head elf?

Receive a brand-new toy as your present?

Winner: | Points:

WOULD YOU RATHER

Be in charge of a Christmas tree farm?

Be in charge of a Christmas turkey farm?

Winner: | Points:

Q 78

Participants:

WOULD YOU RATHER

Have to wash yourself with cranberry sauce?

Have to wash yourself with eggnog?

Q 79

Winner: | Points:

WOULD YOU RATHER

Be the Christmas star and have to sit on top of your Christmas tree?

Be the Christmas tree and have a giant star sit on your head?

Q 80

Winner: | Points:

Participants:

Q 81

WOULD YOU RATHER

Have to untangle a mound of Christmas lights the size of your house?

Have to decorate an entire forest with Christmas lights?

Winner: | Points:

WOULD YOU RATHER

Have to clean up Santa's reindeer stables?

Have to wash all of the elves' clothes?

Winner: | Points:

Q 82

Participants:

WOULD YOU RATHER

Q 83

Receive a present
from a ghost?

Receive a present
from an alien?

Winner: | Points:

WOULD YOU RATHER

Q 84

Have five minutes to get any present
you can find in a store?

Have an hour to get any present you
can find in a regular mall?

Winner: | Points:

Participants:

WOULD YOU RATHER

Go to school on Christmas day and get presents from all your classmates?

Have the entire season of winter off from school but with no Christmas?

Winner: | Points:

Q 85

WOULD YOU RATHER

Visit a candy
cane forest?

Visit a hot chocolate river with marshmallow rocks?

Winner: | Points:

Q 86

Participants:

Q 87

WOULD YOU RATHER

Celebrate Christmas
in the spring?

Celebrate Christmas
in the fall?

Winner:

Points:

WOULD YOU RATHER

Write a new Christmas carol with
Dasher the reindeer?

Write a new Christmas carol with
Mrs. Claus?

Q 88

Winner:

Points:

Participants:

Q 89

WOULD YOU RATHER

Get a gift for Christmas that is a lot of fun for you?

Get a gift for Christmas that is very useful to you?

Winner:

Points:

WOULD YOU RATHER

Have been able to attend Santa Claus and Mrs. Claus's wedding?

Attend a pajama party put on by Santa's elves?

Winner:

Points:

Q 90

Participants:

WOULD YOU RATHER

Celebrate Christmas on Mars with a family of Martians?

Celebrate Christmas in a magical world with fairies and centaurs?

Winner: Points:

Q 91

WOULD YOU RATHER

Cook the Christmas dinner for your family?

Clean up the kitchen after the Christmas dinner is over?

Winner: Points:

Q 92

Participants:

WOULD YOU RATHER

Eat a broccoli-flavoured candy cane?

Drink carrot-flavoured hot chocolate?

Winner: | Points:

Q / 93

WOULD YOU RATHER

Get a picture with Santa Claus that he autographs?

Get a handwritten letter from Santa Claus?

Winner: | Points:

Q / 94

Participants:

WOULD YOU RATHER

Win an ice-skating competition?

Win a sledding competition?

Winner:

Points:

Q 95

WOULD YOU RATHER

Spend Christmas with a family of friendly wolves?

Spend Christmas with a family of playful otters?

Winner:

Points:

Q 96

Participants:

WOULD YOU RATHER

Know exactly what everyone else wants most for Christmas?

Have everyone else know exactly what you want for Christmas?

Winner: Points:

Q 97

WOULD YOU RATHER

Work as an elf in Santa's toy shop?

Become a reindeer and fly Santa's sleigh?

Winner: Points:

Q 98

Participants:

WOULD YOU RATHER

Help the EBI* solve the case of the missing Christmas presents?

Help the EBI* solve the case of the missing Christmas cookies?

Winner: Points:

*(Elf Bureau of Investigations)

Q 99

WOULD YOU RATHER

Be best friends with a living snowman who never melts?

Be best friends with a flying reindeer who can speak English?

Winner: Points:

Q 100

CONGRATULATIONS!

Excellent work! I am sure that there were some obstacles along the way, but you persisted and finished the activities! Hooray!

I also want to give a HUGE THANKS to our staff at Kids Castle Press for making these books a reality. It wouldn't have been possible without them. Feel free to visit our website below to show them some love!

In addition, if you'd like us to send you more free content to print out, you can do so by visiting our website: www.kidscastlepress.com

To add a cherry on top... You can email us for a chance to win a free physical copy of our next book: info@kidscastlepress.com
Don't miss out as we won't be doing this forever... it's a limited time only!

Lastly, if you like this book, would you be so kind as to drop me a review on Amazon?

Thank you very much!

Jennifer L. Trace

TRIVIA PRO CERTIFICATE

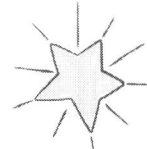

Date: _____   **Signed:** _____

Made in the USA
Coppell, TX
02 December 2021

66983398R00033